ANIMALS GROWING UP™

HOW SEAHORSES GROW UP

Enslow Publishing
101 W. 23rd Street
Suite 240
New York, NY 10011
USA

enslow.com

Linda Bozzo

WORDS TO KNOW

algae Plantlike organisms without leaves or stems that grow in damp or wet places.

camouflage To hide something so it blends in with its surroundings.

coral Sea animals that look like branches and plants.

crustaceans Animals with hard outer shells that usually live in water.

fry A baby seahorse.

hatch To break out of an egg.

larvae Very young forms of animals.

predators Animals that kill and eat other animals to live.

schools Large groups of fish.

shallow Not deep.

CONTENTS

HORSE OR FISH?

Seahorses are not horses at all. They are amazing fish. Seahorses live in shallow, warm water. They may hide in coral. A baby seahorse is called a fry.

FAST FACT

Seahorse babies are born from their fathers, not their mothers!

A colorful little seahorse swims in the ocean. Its face looks like a horse's face!

HATCHED

Like other fish, seahorses hatch from eggs. The father seahorse carries the eggs in his belly pouch until they are ready to hatch. A few to thousands of seahorse fry can be born at a time.

This male's belly is full of eggs. The seahorse and its relatives are the only animals that have the male give birth instead of the female.

FAST FACT

The number of seahorse eggs depends on the type and size of the seahorse.

ON THEIR OWN

Seahorse fry are teeny tiny. Some are only the size of a grain of rice. Once they are born, seahorse fry are on their own!

FAST FACT

Neither the father nor the mother seahorse raise their babies.

Newborn spotted seahorse fry have to take care of themselves!

9

HOLD ON!

A seahorse fry sinks to the bottom of the ocean. Its long tail grabs onto anything it can. Then, it holds on. The hungry fry must begin to catch food.

Seahorses spend most of their time eating.

This yellow seahorse wrapped its tail around some coral so it doesn't drift away.

LOOK OUT!

Seahorse fry must always be on the lookout for predators. Crabs, stingrays, and other fish can eat them. Penguins also make quick meals of seahorse fry.

A seahorse's eyes stick out of its head and can move all around. It would be hard for a predator to sneak up on it!

FAST FACT

A seahorse can move each eye in a different direction to watch for danger.

BLENDING IN

Seahorse fry quickly learn to change color. They must blend in with the world around them. This is how they camouflage themselves to stay safe.

FAST FACT

Unlike other fish, seahorses can swim upright. This makes it easy to hide among plants.

This little red seahorse matches perfectly with the coral it lives in.

SLOW SWIMMERS

A seahorse swims by flapping a tiny fin on its back. This makes seahorses slow swimmers. A seahorse fry will not chase its next meal. It waits for it to pass by.

A seahorse's fins aren't very powerfu[l]
The fish looks like it's just floating
in the water rather than swimming.

FAST FACT

A seahorse has four tiny fins. One fin is on its back. There is a fin on each side of its head. The fourth fin is under its belly.

BIG EATERS

Seahorse fry will eat thousands of crustaceans, such as tiny shrimp. Fry also eat fish larvae, or newly hatched young. The fry sucks in its meal through its long tubelike snout.

FAST FACT

Seahorses have no teeth. The fry learns to swallow its food whole.

A zebra snout seahorse feeds along the ocean bottom.

NO SCHOOL

Many types of fish live in schools, or large groups. But seahorses don't. Most seahorse fry spend their time alone. Some are seen in pairs or small groups.

Three seahorses hang out together. They don't swim in large schools like other fish.

KEEP GROWING

Seahorse fry keep growing their entire lives. Millions of seahorse fry do not survive their first year of life. But certain types of seahorses may live as long as four years in the wild.

Once seahorse fry becor
adults, it's time for them
to find a mate and make
babies of their own.

FAST FACT

A male and female seahorse will dance together
when they meet to make babies.

LEARN MORE

Books

Duhaime, Darla. *Seahorses*. Vero Beach, FL: Rourke Educational Media, 2018.

Hansen, Grace. *Seahorses*. Mankato, MN: Capstone Press, 2017.

Statts, Leo. *Seahorses*. Minneapolis, MN: Abdo Zoom, 2017.

Websites

DKfindout! Seahorses
www.dkfindout.com/us/animals-and-nature/fish/seahorses/
Learn more about seahorses.

National Geographic Kids: Seahorse
kids.nationalgeographic.com/animals/seahorse
Dive deeper into the life of this special fish.

INDEX

Published in 2020 by Enslow Publishing, LLC
101 W. 23rd Street, Suite 240, New York, NY 10011

Copyright © 2020 by Enslow Publishing, LLC

Library of Congress Cataloging-in-Publication Data

Names: Bozzo, Linda, author.
Title: How seahorses grow up / Linda Bozzo.
Description: New York : Enslow Publishing, 2020. | Series: Animals growing up | Includes bibliographical references and index. | Audience: K to Grade 3.
Identifiers: LCCN 2019004752| ISBN 9781978512399 (library bound) | ISBN 9781978512375 (paperback) | ISBN 9781978512382 (6 pack)
Subjects: LCSH: Sea horses—Development—Juvenile literature. | Seahorses—Infancy—Juvenile literature.
Classification: LCC QL638.S9 B69 2020 | DDC 597/.6798—dc23
LC record available at https://lccn.loc.gov/2019004752

Printed in the United States of America

To Our Readers: We have done our best to make sure all website addresses in this book were active and appropriate when we went to press. However, the author and the publisher have no control over and assume no liability for the material available on those websites or on any websites they may link to. Any comments or suggestions can be sent by email to customerservice@enslow.com.

Photos Credits: Cover, p. 1 AshtonEa/Shutterstock.com; interior pages 4-23 (background), p. 15 Fiona Ayerst/Shutterstock.com; p. 5 GOLFX/Shutterstock.com; pp. 7, 13 S.Rohrlach/Shutterstock.com; p. 9 Paulo Oliveira/Alamy Stock Photo; p. 11 Arunee Rodloy/Shutterstock.com; p. 17 Tim_Walters2017/Shutterstock.com; p. 19 Mike Workman/Shutterstock.com; p. 21 Franco Ban/WaterFrame/Getty Images; p. 23 Steven L. Gordon/Shutterstock.com; back cover and additional interior pages background graphic 13Imagery/Shutterstock.com